M000100725

The Piano Songbook

Alicia Keys

ISBN 978-1-4234-8853-8

HAL•LEONARD®
CORPORATION

7777 W. BLUEMOUND RD. P.O. BOX 13819 MILWAUKEE, WI 53213

Visit Hal Leonard Online at
www.halleonard.com

New Arrangements by Olly Weeks and Alex Davis
Edited by Lucy Holliday

AS I AM (INTRO)

Words and Music by Alicia Augello-Cook,
Marsha Ambrosius, Mark Batson and Kerry Brothers Jr

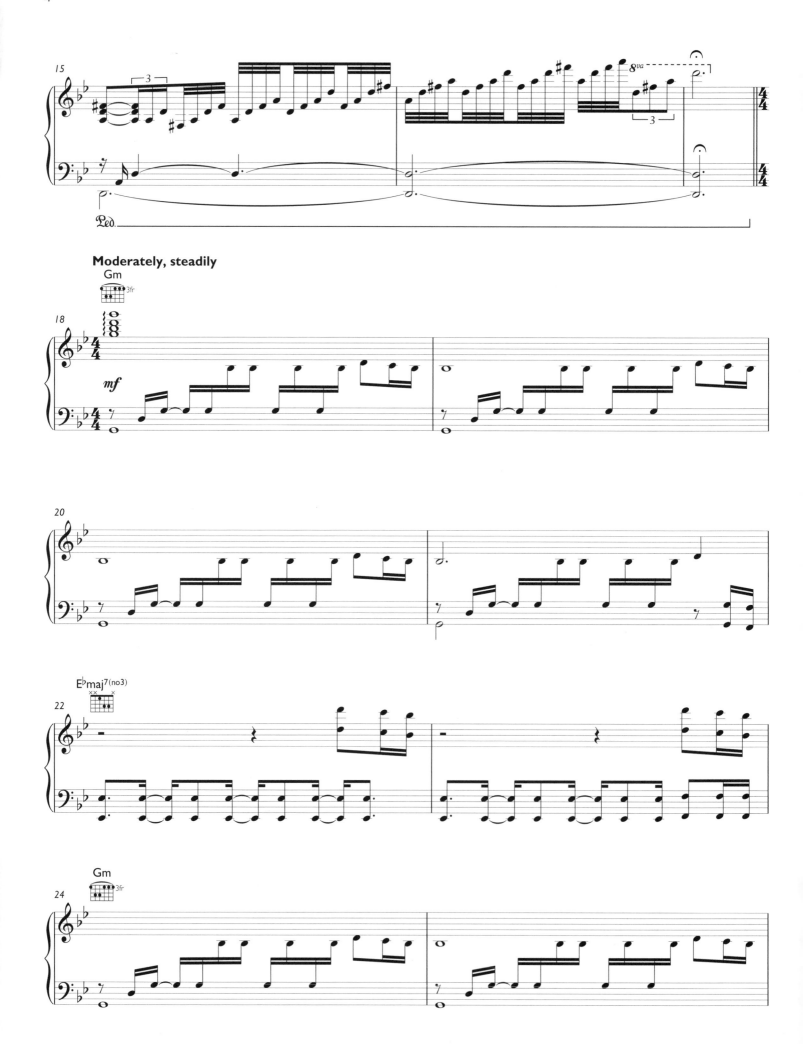

EVERY LITTLE BIT HURTS

Words and Music by Edward Cobb

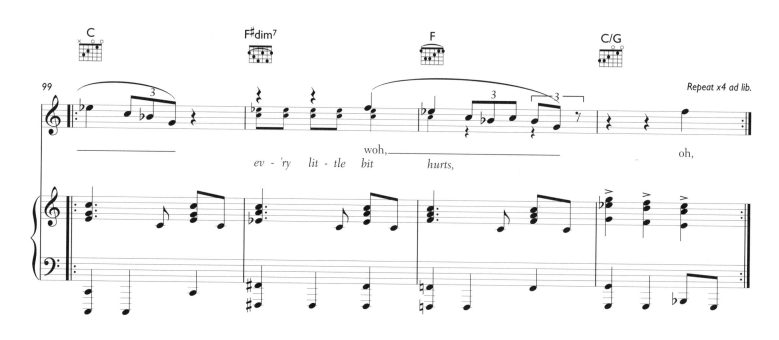

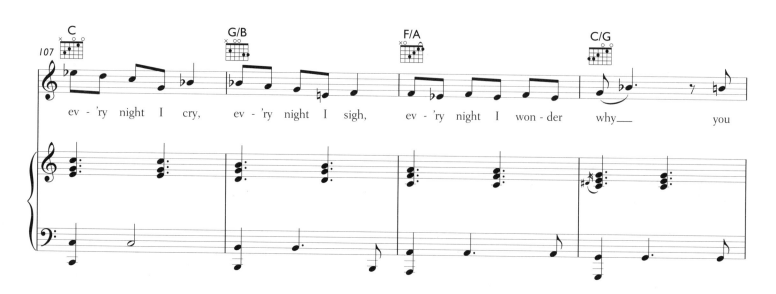

FALLIN'

Words and Music by Alicia Augello-Cook

DRAGON DAYS

Words and Music by Alicia Augello-Cook

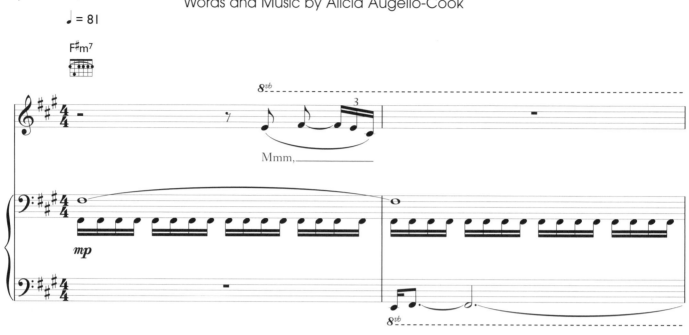

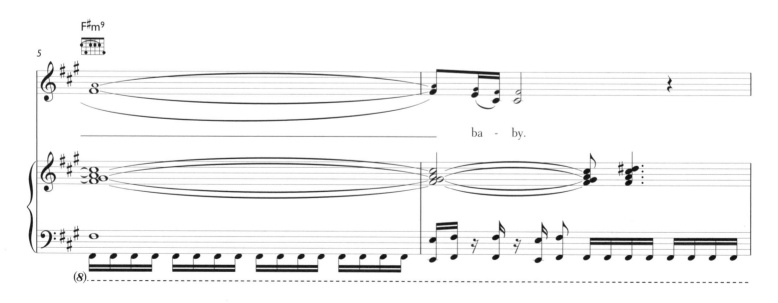

Mmm hmm,___ mmm hmm,___ mmm hmm.___

Mmm hmm,___ mmm hmm,___ mmm hmm.___

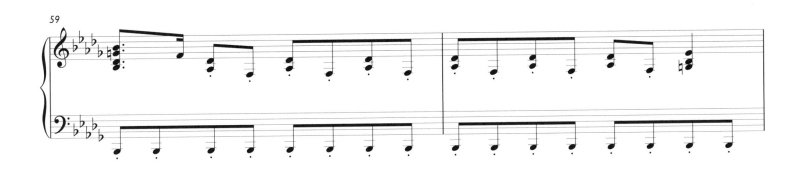

p

HOW COME YOU DON'T CALL ME

Words and Music by Prince Rodgers Nelson

GOODBYE

Words and Music by Alicia Augello-Cook

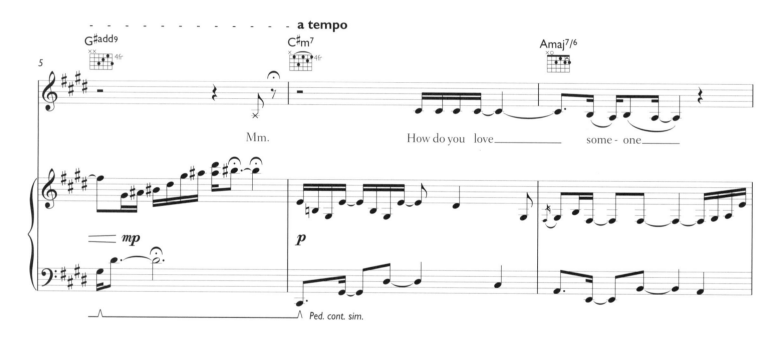

Mm.

How do you love_____ some - one_____

that hurts you, oh so bad?_____

With in - ten -

find the words to say... when your heart don't have the heart to____ say,____ to say____

rit. _ _ _ _ _ _ accel. _ _ _ _ _ _ _ _ _

____ good - bye,_____ find the words to say good-bye?_____

a tempo

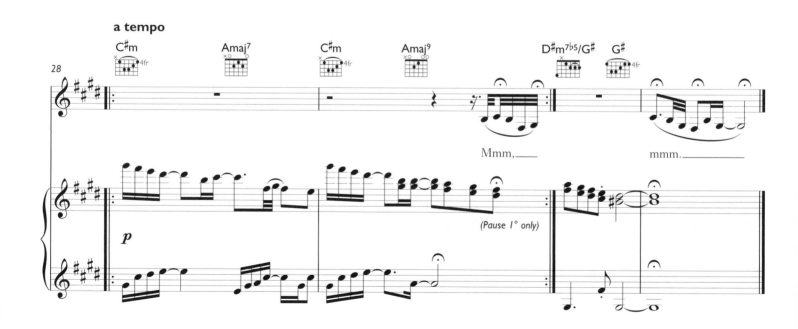

Mmm,____ mmm.

(Pause I° only)

I GOT A LITTLE SOMETHING FOR YOU

Words and Music by Alicia Augello-Cook

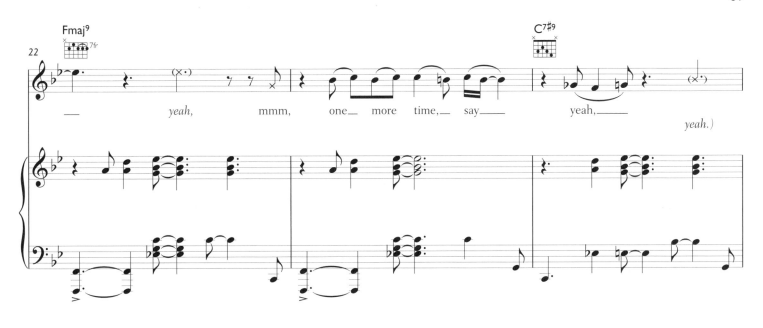

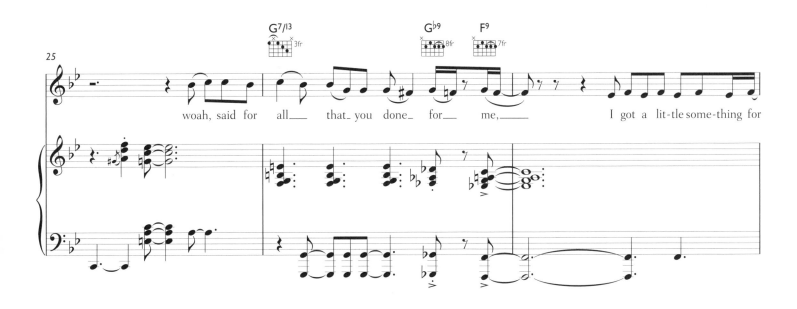

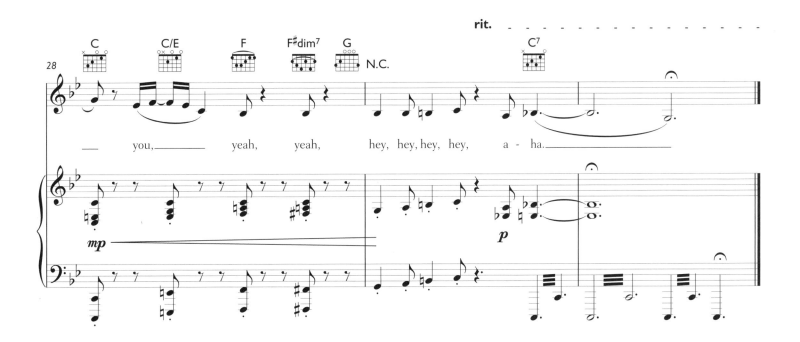

IF I AIN'T GOT YOU

Words and Music by Alicia Augello-Cook

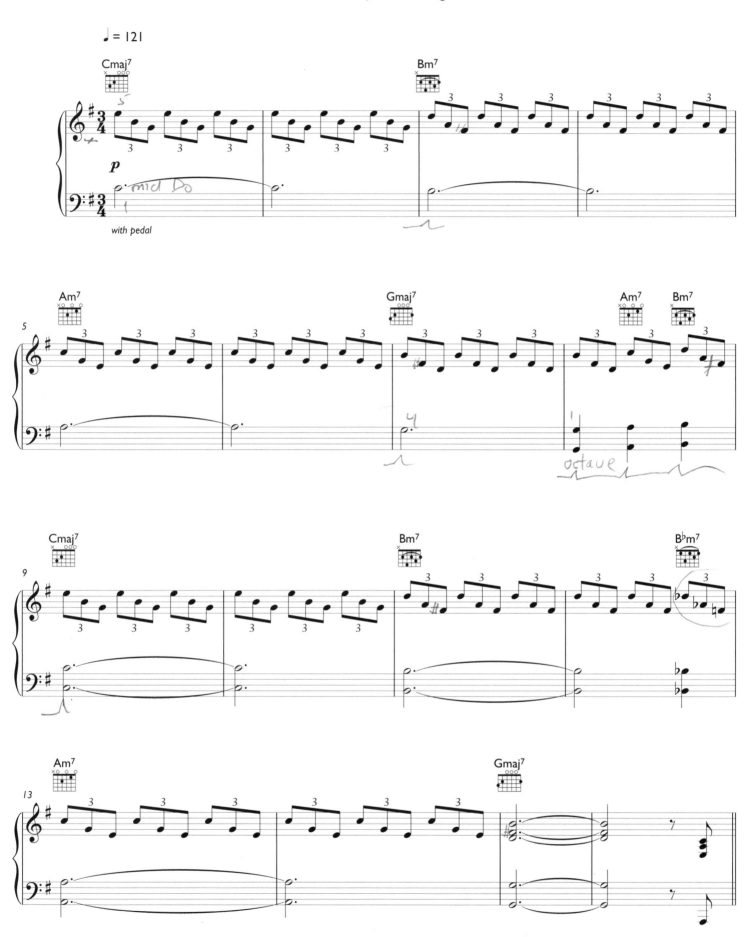

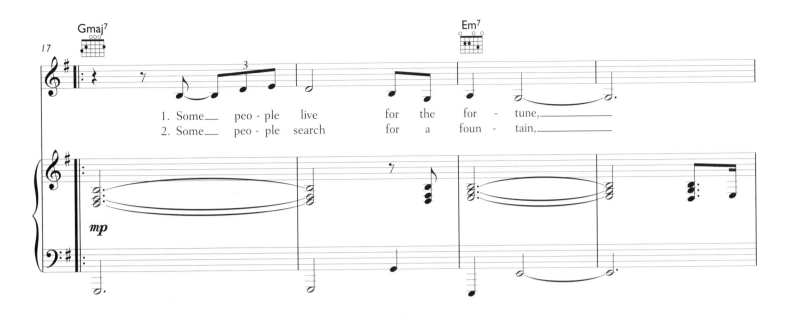

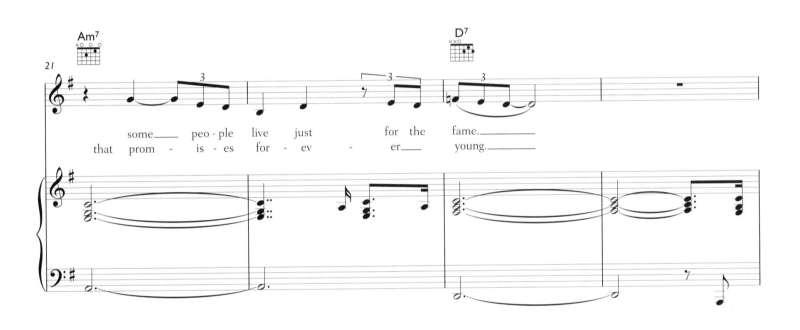

LIKE YOU'LL NEVER SEE ME AGAIN

Words and Music by Alicia Augello-Cook and Kerry Brothers Jr

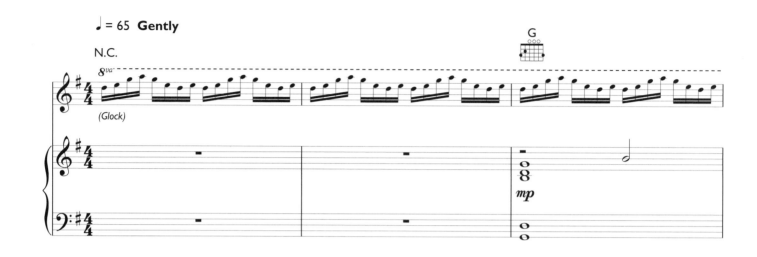

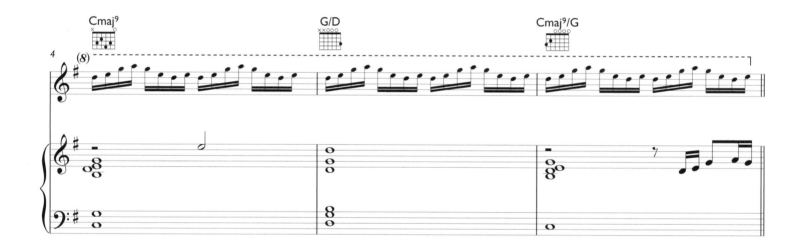

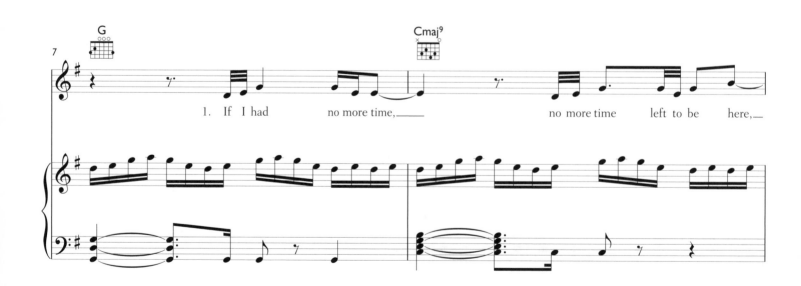

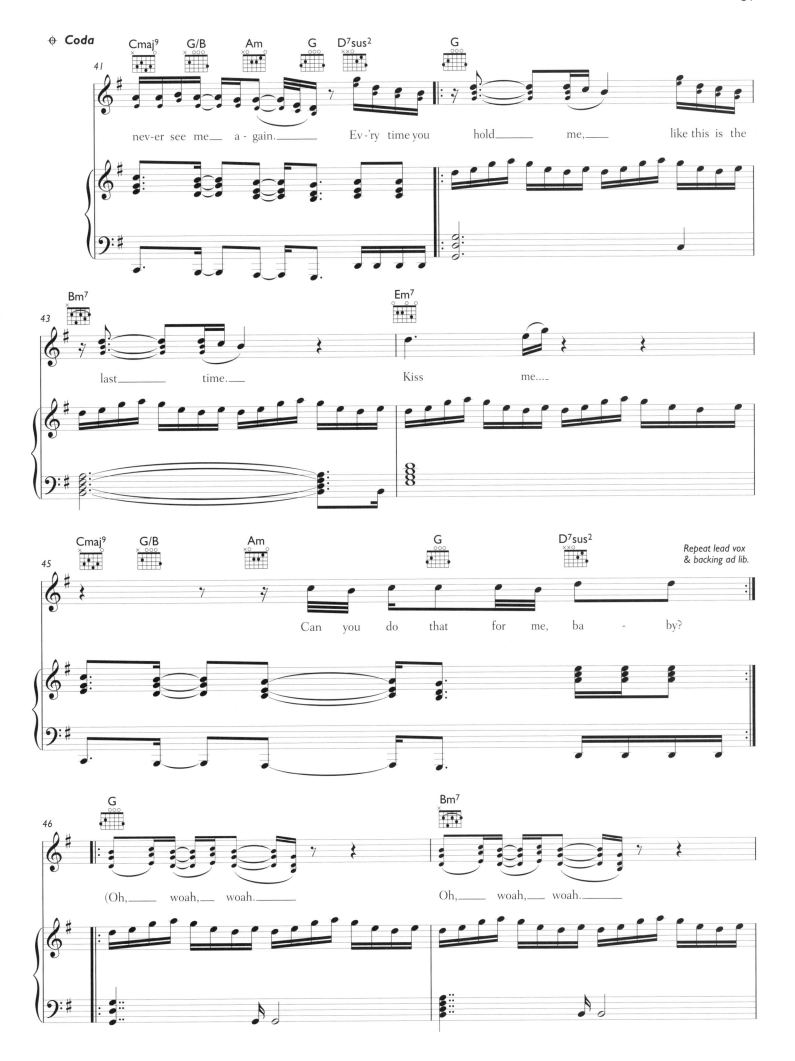

PRELUDE TO A KISS

Words and Music by Alicia Augello-Cook

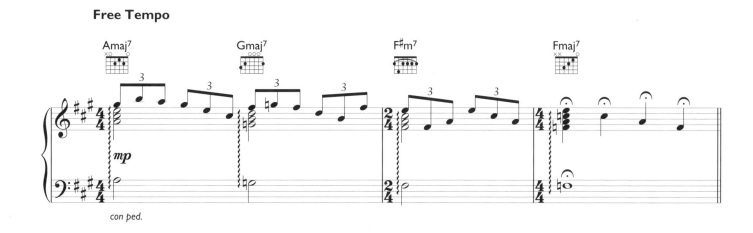

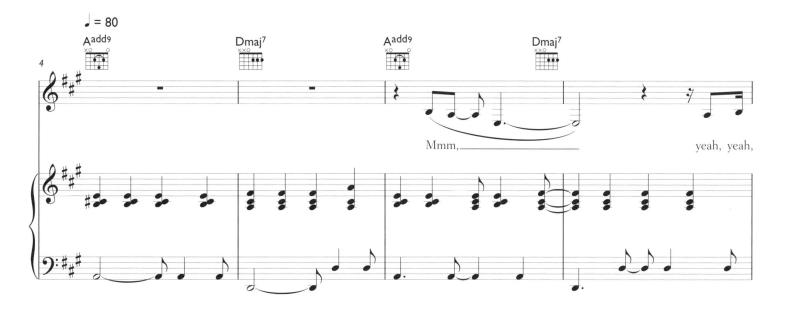

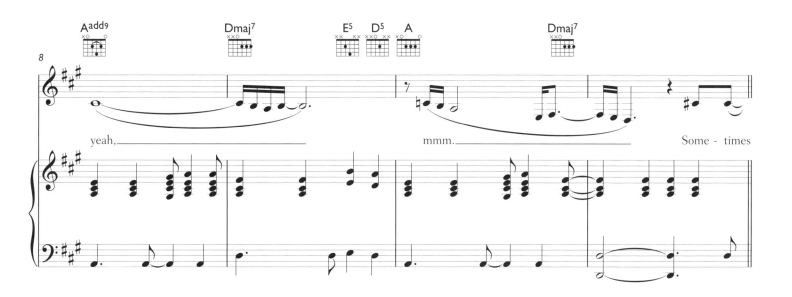

NO ONE

Words and Music by Alicia Augello-Cook,
Kerry Brothers Jr and George Harry

SOMEDAY WE'LL ALL BE FREE

Words and Music by Edward Howard and Donny Hathaway

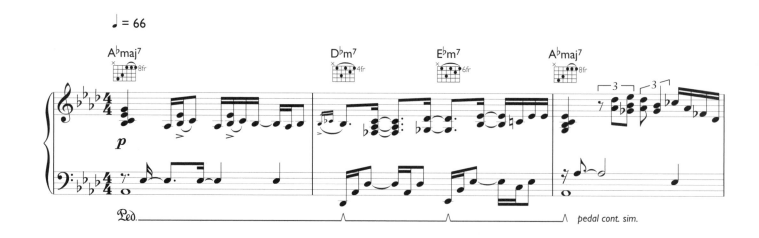

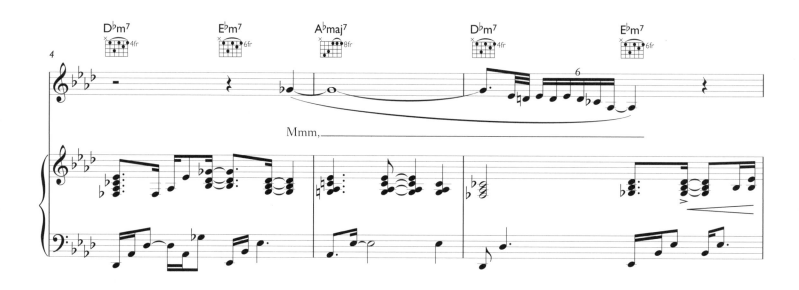

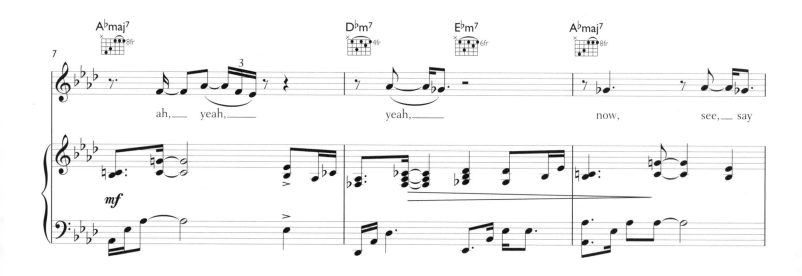

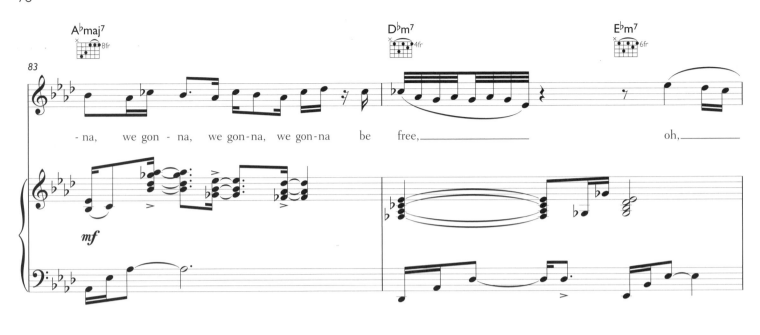

Free tempo

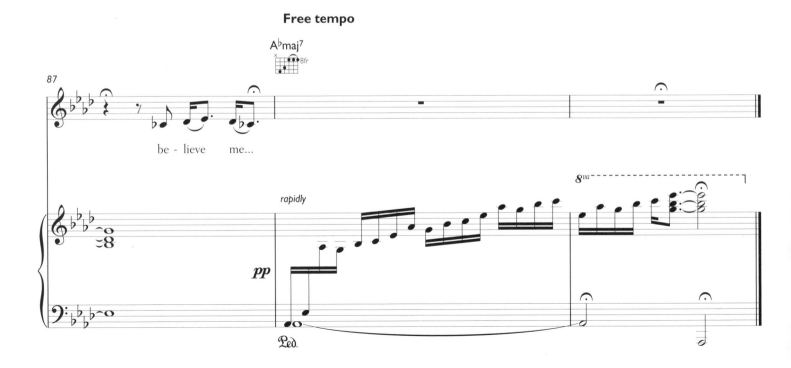

SUPERWOMAN

Words and Music by Alicia Augello-Cook, Linda Perry and Steve Mostyn

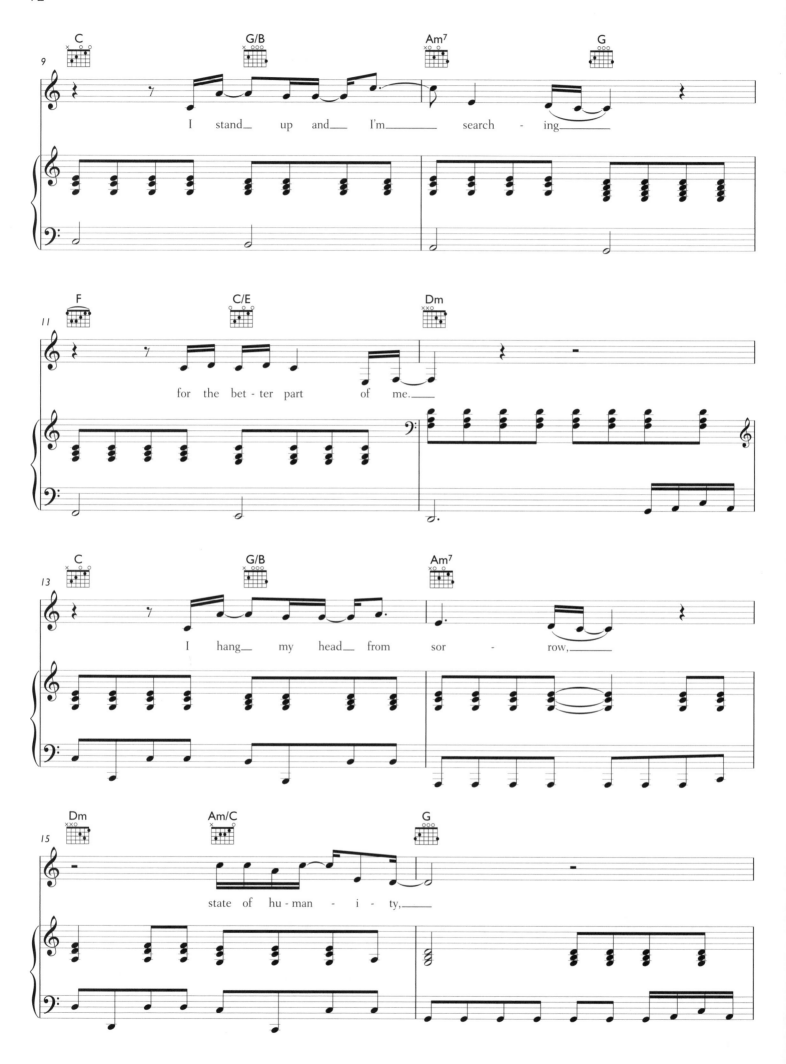

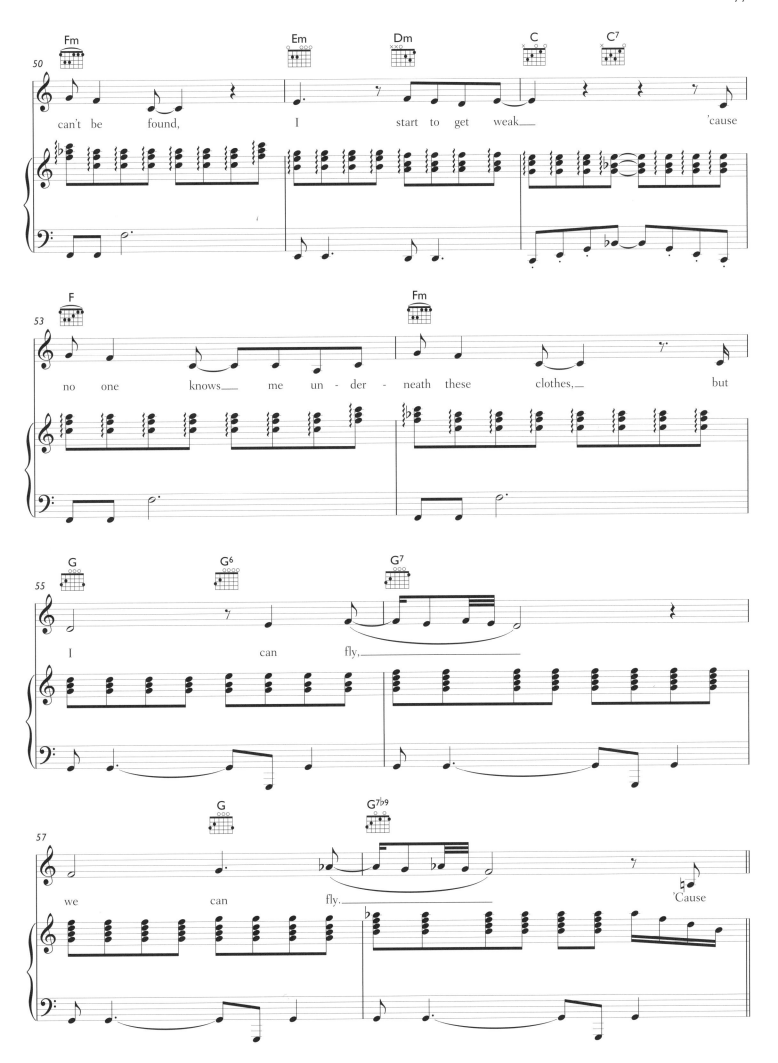

TEENAGE LOVE AFFAIR

Words and Music by Alicia Augello-Cook, Jack Splash, Harold Lilly,
Carl Hampton, Josephine Bridges, Tom Nixon and Matt Kahane

WILD HORSES

Words and Music by Mick Jagger and Keith Richards

WHEN YOU REALLY LOVE SOMEONE

Words and Music by Alicia Augello-Cook and Kerry Brothers Jr

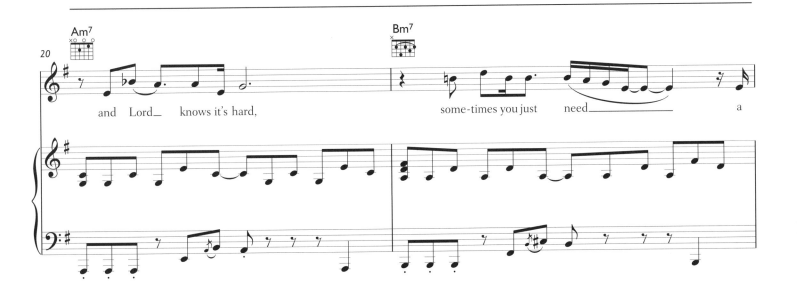

and Lord__ knows it's hard, some-times you just need_____ a

wom-an's touch.____ Sweet af - fec - tion,_____

love_____ and sup - port,_____ when it's real,__ it's un-con-di-tion - al,_____ I'm

A WOMAN'S WORTH

Words and Music by Alicia Augello-Cook and Erika Rose

YOU DON'T KNOW MY NAME

Words and Music by Alicia Augello-Cook, Kanye West,
Harold Lilly, Ralph Bailey, Mel Kent and Ken Williams

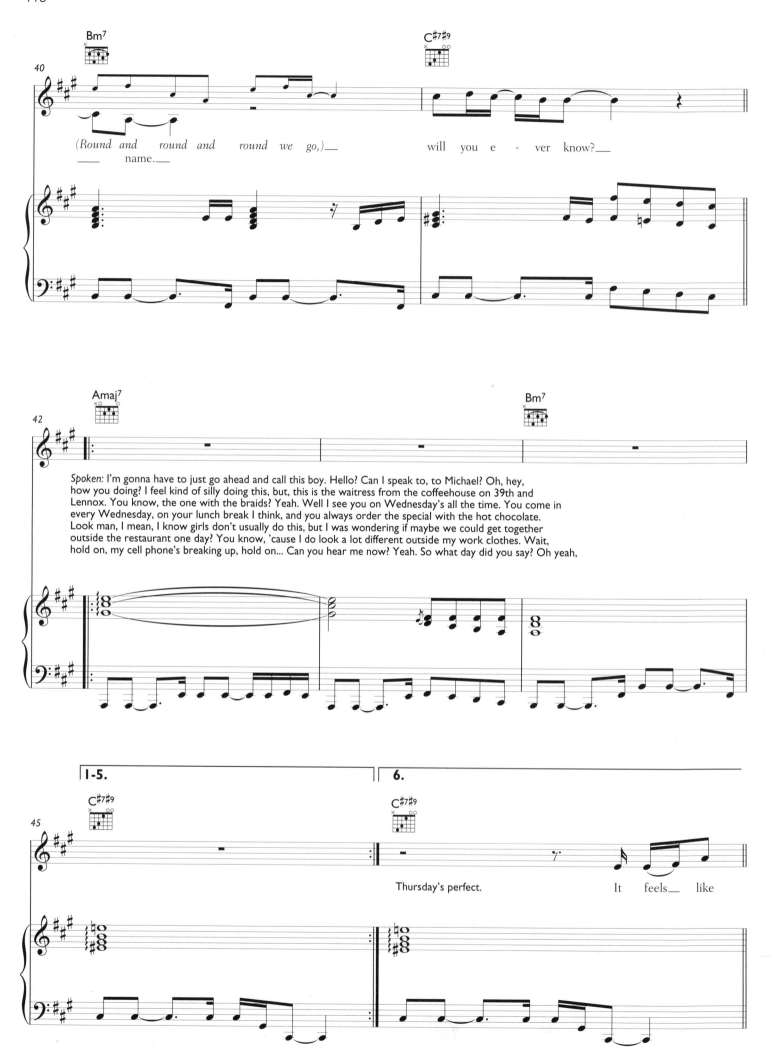